CHOOSING AND USING A CONSULTANT

An Executive Briefing

By Jan Young

CHOOSING AND USING A CONSULTANT

ISBN 978-1-105-37221-6

LOGISTICS

Best Practices in Replenishment of
Forward Pick Locations
>   Options for replenishment and how to
>   choose the best methods

Cycle Count and Physical Inventory
Design and Execution
>   Designing and operating efficient and
>   effective methods

Designing and Using Carousels in
the Warehouse
>   Analyzing operations to design the
>   optimum carousel installation

Selecting, Buying, Installing and
Using a Modern Warehouse Management System
>   The title says it all

Simulation in the Supply Chain
>   What simulation technology can and
>   cannot do in the supply chain

Supply Chain Metrics
>   How to measure and monitor supply
>   chain operations

FICTION

Mom and Me
>   Three novellas prominently featuring
>   cats

Claude
>   A novel of the distant future

Eternity
>   A life in heaven is not a bed of roses

TRAVEL

Northwest USA by RV
>   Our 2010 travel to Oregon and Wash-
>   ington with lots of other stops, all in
>   full color

Missouri and Maine by RV
>   Two trips in 2009, one to Missouri
>   and one to Maine in full color

Alaska by RV
>   Our 2008 trip to Alaska, western
>   Canada and the northwestern USA in
>   full color

Atlantic Coast by RV
>   2011 travel through Alabama to
>   Georgia and the Carolinas

CARS AND TRAINS

Studebaker and the Railroads
>   A two volume history of the Stude-
>   baker Corporation of South Bend,
>   Indiana, railroading in the South
>   Bend area, and connections between
>   them

Tales of Studebaker: The Early
Years
>   Historic sidelights and illuminating
>   stories about the company and the
>   people

History of the American Automobile
Industry
>   Reprint of a 1916 history written by
>   the editor of *The Automobile*, David
>   Beecroft

The Studebaker History Corner
>   More than a hundred short historic
>   stories about Studebaker

Studebaker Bibliography
>   A catalog of almost five thousand
>   books and articles about Studebaker

History of the Studebaker Corporation
>   Reprint of a rare 1918 book by Albert
>   Erskine, Studebaker's President

TW and ASR Indexes
>   Indexes of the content of Turning
>   Wheels and Antique Studebaker Re-
>   view magazines

The Life of Clement Studebaker
>   Reprint of a biography believed to
>   have been written by Ann Studebaker
>   after his death

GENERAL INTEREST

State Flags of the United States
>   Images, symbolism and history of the
>   US state and territorial flags in full
>   color

The United States Constitution
>   The history and content of the US
>   Constitution and its amendments

Thirty Years as a Volunteer Treas-
urer
>   What I learned as a church treasurer

Our Ancestry
>   A three volume set listing almost
>   twelve thousand people

The Assassins
>   Forty-six historic stories of murder
>   and mayhem on a global scale

Table of Contents

Introduction

Purpose of this Paper

There's an old joke: Why is a consultant like a seagull? Answer: They fly into town, mess all over everything, and fly out!

There's more than a little truth in that joke. Consultants, by their nature, are temporary and to get the best available, management often hires on a national or even a global scale. The more a company needs consulting help, the more changes the consultant is likely to recommend, and thus the more he or she is likely to be viewed as a troublemaker by the people who do the work and have been doing it for years.

Consultants, actually, are much more than the joke implies: they bring in exper-tise that is otherwise unavailable and usually – but not always -- contribute much more than they cost. So, the pur-pose of this paper is to familiarize the reader with the concepts behind consult-ing, with the nature of the consulting marketplace, and with the plusses and minuses involved.

About the Author

Jan Young is a trained Industrial Engineer with thirty-eight years experience in manufacturing and distribution. Now retired, he has:

o Managed a factory and a warehouse employing over a hundred workers in a 24/7/365 continuous operation

o Sold, installed, configured and maintained both manufacturing planning and warehouse management systems on a global scale for more than thirty years

o Designed a warehouse management system. That system, aimed at the top-tier market, was one of the premier commercially-available systems when introduced

o Consulted in more than fifty warehouses and factories in ten countries

What is a Consultant?

A consultant is just like an employee, but one that comes without responsibility for payroll taxes or benefits and without the need to make a legal or ethical commitment to retain him or her after a project is complete. Consultants also often work without any investment on your part in office space or equipment. Typically they are more self-directed and better motivated than employees.

A good consultant will have all of the attributes of a good employee: skill, energy, resources, loyalty, honesty, punctuality, and availability. But when the job is done, the expense stops. The trick to hiring and effectively using a consultant lies in the fact that, like employees, not all consultants deliver on all jobs.

Why Use a Consultant?

Consultants are useful when you need skills that aren't on your staff or aren't on your staff in sufficient quantity. Sometimes this happens when there is insufficient work to keep a person with certain skills busy full time and there is no opportunity to combine those skills with similar work to make an attractive full time job. It also happens when there is just too much going on and your existing staff simply can't get needed projects done in the time available.

The advantages to using a consultant, therefore, are:

1. You can get more done in less time

2. You can to do some kinds of work that could not otherwise be done because the requisite skills are not available or not available in sufficient quantity on your staff

3. You can get work done sooner by using consultants to supplement existing staff

4. You can avoid the long term commitments made to employees

5. Consultants are frequently more objective and more credible than staff members

However, the disadvantages of consultants are:

1. Your short term costs may be increased depending, in part, on how those costs are measured

2. You incur a risk of non-performance or poor performance by an unknown or untested consultant. This risk, however, is probably lower than when hiring.

Differences in Consulting Firms

Essentially all consultants either own or work for corporations, with Limited Liability Corporations (LLCs) and S-Corporations being the most common forms. You will, therefore, be contracting with a corporation and not an individual.

There are, of course, large, medium and small consulting firms. The consulting industry is more fragmented than most, meaning that there are more medium sized and small firms than you might expect. Different size firms have different advantages and disadvantages.

> ➢ Large firms have, of course, the capacity to take on large projects with possibly dozens of people at work at one time. They tend to have been in business for many years and have extensive references. They can usually offer a broad range of skills and can sometimes provide significant depth in selected skills.
>
> Large firms, however, tend to have significant overhead and thus higher rates than smaller firms. They also tend to have large customer bases and thus are often less interested in small projects and in projects from

one-time customers. A small or medium sized customer tends to be a number to a large consulting firm and there may thus be more distraction and thus less loyalty and less dedication to the job.

➢ Medium sized firms (those with between three and ten consultants) are significantly more flexible than large firms, but tend to be narrower in their scope. Some medium sized firms are actually small firms that have enough volume to employ a significant number of non-consulting analysts.

➢ Small firms (one or two consultants) offer the ultimate in flexibility, but at the cost of relatively narrow scope, although their skills may be very deep. Small firms tend strongly to bond with their clientele and to be very loyal, especially when the clients are loyal to them. Because small firms have little or no overhead, their rates tend to be the lowest and when a good skill match is possible, they can offer the best value on the market. However, this value can be offset if the principal (or principals) lack experience as business people or if they get out of their depth in a project.

Most small consulting firms, on the other hand, spend a great deal of energy building relationships with other small consultants. These relationships allow them to call on each other, to support each other when necessary, and even to subcontract with each other to provide special services, to cover larger projects, and to add to their skill sets. Alliances such as these allow small consulting firms to act, for many purposes, like much larger firms.

Consulting firms vary greatly by specialization and the skills and knowledge they offer to the market. Since there are tens (or possibly hundreds) of thousands of consultants in the US, finding one or two with the exact skill set you need is only a matter of searching.

Consultants can also be characterized geographically. For some projects, you may prefer a consultant who is based nearby and can drop in on an informal basis whenever necessary. For other projects, however, where the consultant is based can be almost irrelevant. E-mail, cell phones and online video conferencing can make long distances seem much shorter.

And possibly the most important difference between one consulting firm and the next is their experience. The best consultants are experienced business people as well as being experienced in their own technical specialty, so they can work smoothly with you on contracting issues, and can discuss liability and conflict of interests and other business details easily and accurately. The best also have experience in numerous industries and can cross-fertilize by bringing ideas from one to another.

Cost of Consulting Services

M ost industrial consultants charge from $75 to $500 per hour, depending on their skills, the amount of competition in their market, and on how badly they want work. That sounds like a lot, but remember the following:

➢ The consultant pays his or her own payroll taxes including Social Security, Medicare and unemployment. These taxes take 20% off the top.

➢ The consultant pays his or her own benefits including health insurance, pension, vacations, holidays, and more. These costs can easily take another 30% of the fees.

➢ The consultant pays for his or her overhead including office space, telephones, support staff, and computers and software.

➢ The consultant must also cover his or her selling time for which he isn't paid. In small shops without a professional sales force, the typical consultant easily spends half of his time selling. This cuts the effective take-home pay in half yet again.

Choosing and Using a Consultant

All in all, the consultant who charges $100 per hour is lucky to take home a quarter of it, and if he or she works in a large firm with management overhead, the net income can be even less. And remember that these numbers are before income taxes. Many consultants manage to live comfortably, but only a few get rich.

Some consultants publish rate schedules, but many do not. In fact, the rates charged by most consultants vary with their assessment of the risk and the overhead involved in a specific project.

For instance, a one-week project with vaguely defined goals done for a new customer where there is no pre-existing relationship will represent a high level of risk to the consultant, particularly if he is asked to quote a fixed price for the work. Since the short duration means a high ratio of selling to billing hours, and since the risk of non-payment or the possibility of extensive collection efforts is high with a new and unknown customer, the consultant will ask top dollar. On the other hand, a longer project with well defined goals done on an hourly rate basis for an existing customer who is known to pay promptly will represent a low risk situation and will motivate the consultant to price as competitively as possible.

Choosing and Using a Consultant

Most consultants bill their expenses in addition to their time and most bill expenses as incurred, but some add mark-ups.

Generally consultants price their time based on one of five models:

> ➤ Hourly rates

> Billing based on the number of hours actually worked is the most common method used by general business consultants. They like the hourly rate billing model because it protects them from customer-driven scope changes and removes the risk that they may have to do unforeseen work at no charge.

> From the vantage point of the client, the advantage of hourly rated consulting is that the absolute rates are likely to be lower (since the consultant will view the risk as lower). The disadvantage, of course, is that the client assumes the risk of the project being larger or more complex than anticipated.

> Another disadvantage, of course, is the risk that the consultant will bill hours not spent on the project, or will spend hours doing unnecessary

work. Ethical consultants will not do either of these things, but the customer takes the risk.

➢ Fixed price

Many consulting clients are concerned about paying based on the actual hours worked by the consultant because they have only minimal control over how the consultant spends his or her time. Some (but not all) consultants are willing to work for a fixed project price, but most will require a detailed and firm project specification.

While clients often perceive fixed price projects as more advantageous, the fixed-price pricing model may or may not actually be better. If the client is confident that the scope of the project is clearly defined and that it will not change, fixing the price may actually result in a higher cost.

➢ Capped hourly rates

Anticipating or reacting to client reservations about straight hourly billing, many consultants will propose based on an hourly rate with a cap or ceiling. The definition of what will happen when the ceiling is reached varies. Some consulting firms will continue to completion if the project on a non-billable basis. Others will simply cease work.

In either case, the client should be concerned that a project billing cap could affect the quality of the consultant's work. If, for example, the consultant see that it will not be possible to complete the project within the capped amount of time, there will be great temptations on his or her part to find shortcuts to reduce the time investment. These shortcuts may or may not affect the quality of the final product.

➤ Contract employee

A contract employment arrangement is one under which the consultant works on a hourly rate, but without responsibility for the favorable or unfavorable outcome of the project. Like an employee, he or she simply follows the client's directions and works (more or less) a predefined number of hours per week. The advantage of this arrangement to clients is that the consultant takes little or no risk and therefore will work for much lower rates than if he or she were taking risk. The disadvantage is that consultants working as contract employees require more supervision.

➢ Gainsharing

In rare circumstances, consultants will work for a predefined percentage of the benefits the client receives from the project rather than for a fixed sum or hourly rate. So if, for instance, the project's goal is to reduce labor cost, the consultant might agree to do the work for 50% of the first year's actual savings.

From the consultant's viewpoint, this is a high risk model and, from the client's viewpoint, it is relatively low risk. Most consultants, before accepting gainsharing work, will insist on a significant measure of control over the project and the resources required to complete it, will want a detailed definition of how the gains will be measured, and will want a percentage of the gains that, if achieved, will be highly profitable. The administrative effort and the cost of gain measurement often make gainsharing less attractive.

Your Consulting Project

Before you start to look for a consultant, define what you want the consultant to do in the form of a preliminary project specification. This document should address at least the following topics:

> ➢ The goals and objectives you want the project to accomplish

> ➢ The skills and time required to meet these goals and objectives, as best you understand the work to be done

> ➢ How the work should be divided between an outside consultant and your existing staff

> ➢ Your perception of the financial value of achieving the goals and objectives (this statement helps put the cost of the consultants in perspective)

> ➢ Your desired timeline for the project

Some firms who use consultants regularly believe that a consultant should be retained not only to identify and specify solutions, but also to implement and support them. Generally these beliefs are founded on the idea that total responsibility for a project will make the consultants more realistic and will provide better results. Other firms, however, rely on consultants primarily for their experience and creativity. These firms feel that they can reduce cost by using internal resources to manage implementations, work which requires significantly less creativity. The choice of whether you engage a consultant to carry through is subjective and is up to you, but you should be aware of the alternatives.

How to Find and Choose The Right Consultant

Consultants can usually be found using a variety of directories, Internet searches, and lists from associations and professional societies. Vendors may be able to make referrals (or may be candidates themselves). Customers and other associates with similar businesses or similar business issues often can also refer or recommend consulting firms.

Begin by making a list of consulting firms that appear to have the skills you need. Then make initial telephone contact with the firms on your list and verify verbally that they have the appropriate skills in the appropriate amounts and that they are available to do the work in the time available.

Select a small number of consultants who appear the most desirable and invite them to interview for the work. During the interview, focus on their skills and background and ask enough questions to assure yourself:

➤ That they understand the issues you are facing,

➢ That they share your feeling that the project has merit,

➢ That they understand the technologies that will be needed to resolve the issues,

➢ That they have the capacity to accomplish your work in a reasonable time,

➢ That they have the communication skills required to understand the work to be done and to properly present their results,

➢ That they have done this work or similar work before with success, and

➢ That their standard contractual terms are within reason.

Winnow the list after the interviews and establish a specification for the job. Your specification may be different for different candidates, depending on their skills and what you want them to do. Write your specification into the form of a Request for Proposal (RFP).

In addition to the job specification, the RFP should state the pricing model you want and alternatives you will accept. It

should also require the consultant to
specify the individual people who will be
doing (or at least leading) the work and
should require that you have an opportunity to meet and interview these people if
you haven't done so already.   Accept the
fact that the consulting firm has other
commitments and allow it to time-bind its
commitment.   Because it is critical that
the consultants (or at least the consulting
project manager) be someone you know,
have evaluated and trust, your RFP
should reserve the right to cancel the contract if this person is not assigned and if
your project is not his or her primary project during its life.

You should expect to pay for the consultants travel expenses. The RFP should require the bidder to state whether expenses
will be billed at cost or will be marked up.
Also ask if expenses will include anything
other than travel (such as telephone costs,
office staff, copying, etc.).

Your RFP should require references, but it
should also commit to your bidders that
reference checking will be the last thing
done and will only be done for the two
leading contenders. Consultants guard
their reference fiercely and rightfully so.

And finally, your RFP should request that
the consultant include a copy of his writ-

ten statement of ethics in his or her proposal. While it is true that anyone can write a statement of ethics and then ignore it, comparison with the model statement in Appendix A will give you some indication of the degree to which the consultant takes his or her ethical position seriously.

Then get quotes from the chosen consultants.

Select the consultant you will use based partly on the quoted price, but also weigh your level of confidence in the firm and your relationship with the people you have met least as heavily as the price. All too often, the low bidder either does not understand the problem fully, or is desperate to get the work.

It is almost never wise to choose a consultant based on price alone. In fact, in view of the risks and the size of many consulting projects, cost is often a minor consideration.

As you choose your consultant:

> ➢ Be careful about taking on ex-employees as consultants unless they are in the consulting business and understand consulting as a profession. It is not a part-time job.

Choosing and Using a Consultant

The ex-employee consultant may have the exact mix of skills you need and may be capable of coming up to speed on a project quickly, but will almost certainly act like an employee and you will loose the benefits of broad multi-company experience and independence.

➢ Also be careful of consultants who are introduced to you by luminaries of one kind or another including well-known college professors, high-ranking association officials and other similar people. There is a good possibility that these people have been directly or indirectly paid to promote the consulting company. You should, at least, verify that the recommender received no compensation in any form for the recommendation.

➢ Your consultant should disclose to you his relationship with everyone who is working on your project. You should not be surprised if some are subcontractors and not employees of the consulting firm, but the relationships should be known and above board. You should ask for copies of agreements between the consultant and any subcontractors.

Choosing and Using a Consultant

➤ You should be concerned if your consultant sells or attempts to sell you something other than pure consulting services. While material-handling firms, for example, can perform valid and valuable consulting in their field, there are obvious biases and you may be better served with a consultant who is objective.

➤ And finally, your chosen consultant should disclose to you any referral fees or other payments that have been made to promote or protect his position in your bidding process. He or she should also disclose any non-compete agreements he has with other firms.

Contracting

A model contract is attached as Appendix B. However, this contract in its current version has not been reviewed by any attorney and is not specific with regard to state law. It must not be used directly, but can serve as a source of ideas and for comparison with the contract that your chosen consultant will doubtlessly provide.

Do not employ a consultant without a written contract.

The best consulting contracts act as an umbrella, providing a contracting relationship, but without definition of the work to be done. They provide for separate Statements of Work (SOWs) to define the project or projects to be done.

The Statement of Work for a project should be in writing and should be signed by both the consultant and the customer, but it can be less formal and less structured than the contractual agreement itself.

The SOW can be written by you, the client, or by the consultant, although the consultant will normally want to be the author. Either way, the SOW should be carefully reviewed and approved by both parties. It should include:

- ➢ A description of project objectives, usually in non-numeric, qualitative terms

- ➢ A list of project objectives in numeric, quantitative terms where possible – but this list should be limited to real objectives and should not include numbers just for the sake of having numbers.

- ➢ A description or list of the facilities where project work will be done

- ➢ A project scope or a list of boundaries; definition of work that is included and work that is excluded

- ➢ A description of project phases or stages to the extent that they are necessary

- ➢ A list of specific tasks the consultant will do. This list need not be complete, but should cover everything the client thinks is important. Its purpose is to verify that the consultant thinks those items are important too.

- ➢ A list of specific tasks or responsi-
  bilities of the client. This list recog-
  nizes that few consulting jobs can
  be done in a vacuum. It serves to
  assure that you (the client company)
  are prepared to do your share.

- ➢ A description of the methods or
  methodologies that the consultant
  will follow, if they are important to
  the client.

- ➢ A project schedule, possibly with
  specific dates but more likely defin-
  ing a sequence of activities and generally expected dates.

  - o Despite the fact that individ-
    ual tasks may not have spe-
    cific scheduled dates, mile-
    stones should be established
    and expected dates for each
    should be agreed upon

  - o The schedule should define
    the total project duration and
    an expected completion date,
    possibly with a tolerance.

- ➢ A list of project deliverables. Deliverables commonly include a final
  report and an accompanying pres-
  entation

➢ Definition of the work papers that the consultant is to create and maintain, at least to the extent that these work papers are likely to be important to the client

➢ Definition of the specific personnel (some or all) to be used on the project. Also, if important, definition of the total number of people who will be available to work on the project as needed.

➢ Definition of the customer's personnel (some or all) to be used on the project and definition of their schedule and the extent to which they will be available for project work.

➢ Definitions of other project resources that the client will be required to provide (e. g. computers, software, equipment, information, documentation, etc.). If significant, definitions of similar resources that the consultant will provide.

➢ A statement of total estimated project cost, listing expenses and fees separately. This statement may require qualifications and/or a list of assumptions and conditions.

Choosing and Using a Consultant

➢ A specification for progress reports that the consultant will prepare (both report frequency and report content)

➢ A space for formal signature by both parties.

Post-Contract

The very best consultants will see to it that you will get value from your consulting project regardless of how well you manage the project. However, at the outset of a project, you have no certain way of knowing whether or not you have hired the best, so it is incumbent on you to proactively manage the consultant and the consulting relationship.

For most consulting projects, you should name an internal project manager whose responsibility will be to act as primary interface to the consulting organization and to facilitate their work as necessary. In some instances you may elect to do this work yourself, depending on the availability of other people and the sensitivity of the work to be done.

Before the project actually starts, be sure you can measure progress and results. Determine how you want to measure the results, make sure that your decision is consistent with the Statement of Work, and perform a baseline measurement so you have numbers to compare to when the project is complete.

Every consulting project should begin with a kickoff meeting. The kickoff meeting should be attended by the consultant and as many of his or her staff as practical. The client's sponsoring manager and project manager should also attend along with as many of the people who will be working directly with the consultant as possible. In instances in which the consultant will be working on a factory or warehouse floor in view of the workforce, supervisors should also attend.

The purpose of the kickoff meeting should be communication and coordination, to make sure that everyone understands what is being done, why it is being done, how the work will proceed, and what the expected outcome is. The meeting can be relatively short. The agenda might consist of:

➢ Introduction of the consulting firm, the consultant's project manager, and the consulting staff

➢ Introduction of key client personnel

➢ Explanation of who, why, where, what, when and how by the sponsoring manager

➢ Review of the Statement of Work (possibly excluding financial details)

➢ Open the floor for questions

Choosing and Using a Consultant

The internal project manager should monitor progress as the project proceeds and this monitoring should be done independently of the consultant's written progress reports. He or she should assure that the project is on schedule and should ask questions when evidence of proper project performance is absent.

The internal project manager should also track promises and commitments made by the consultant and note which ones were met and which were not. An early pattern of missed dates and incomplete work is a bad sign.

And most importantly, the project manager should guard against scope creep. Scope creep is the common tendency for projects to expand as work is done, taking on new objectives and addressing new issues. It often results from poor project definition, sometimes coupled with the consultant's natural tendency to want more work and more billing. There can be instances in which project expansion is necessary and justifiable, but the changes should be documented in the form of a signed revision to the Statement of Work and should be approved by the proper people.

Appendix A – Model Ethics Statement

CLIENT INTERESTS

➤ (Name of consulting firm) conducts all consultations and related business in a manner that unequivocally places the interest of the client first.

➤ We closely guard the confidentiality of business information provided by our clients.

➤ We do not consult with two competing businesses at the same time without the full knowledge and approval of all concerned.

➤ Even if the projects are not simultaneous, we do not disclose information about one client's business to another competing client.

➤ We do not accept consultations that create or could create conflicts of interest with our other business or personal interests or financial activities, or those of our families.

➤ We promptly report facts encountered and assumptions made during our work when there is the possibility that the quality or reliability of our work has been or could be compromised.

COMPENSATION

➤ Our sole compensation for a consulting project is client invoicing.

➤ All time-based billing is based on actual logged hours of work. Logs are limited to time actually worked and, unless agreed otherwise with the client, do not include time spent on administrative work, travel, or other activities not directly related to the client's project.

➤ We do not accept fees, commissions, kickbacks or things of value from third parties who we recommend to our clients. Similarly, we do not recommend any third parties in which we have a financial interest.

PERSONAL CONDUCT

➤ We conduct ourselves professionally at all times when on the client site and when in communication with the client.

➤ We respect and observe the law, making all disclosures expected by the law and the consulting profession

➢ We make great efforts to meet all commitments on time and within budget and when it becomes evident that the available time and/or budget are inadequate, immediately contact the client and seek guidance.

➢ We respect our clients and do not make public statements that devalue or appear to devalue them or their business. We respect our clients' employees and value their contributions.

➢ We do not represent our clients to others as endorsing or recommending our services without obtaining prior permission. We do not use our clients as references without obtaining prior permission.

➢ We do not discriminate against any person or organization based on race, color, national origin, sex, age, religion, marital status, handicap or citizenship.

➢ We do not engage in any form of sexual harassment.

Appendix B – Model Consulting Contract

To reiterate, this contract was not written by an attorney and we are not presenting it as an executable, legal document. The reader should use it as a source of ideas only.

Footnotes in this appendix are explanatory and should not be considered to be part of the agreement itself.

CONSULTING AGREEMENT

This AGREEMENT is made and entered into as of (Date) by and between _____ ("Customer"), and _____ ("Consultant") with offices located respectively at _____ and _____.

WHEREAS, CONSULTANT is in the business of providing consultation and technical support services and

WHEREAS, CUSTOMER desires to engage CONSULTANT for the Project described in the Statement of Work

NOW, THEREFORE, in consideration of the promises and mutual agreements herein, CUSTOMER and CONSULTANT agree as follows:

Choosing and Using a Consultant

CONSULTANT's Engagement

CUSTOMER hereby engages CONSULTANT and CONSULTANT agrees to be so engaged on the terms and conditions set forth in this Agreement to perform a consulting project described more specifically in one or more Statements of Work ("SOW") in a form similar to Attachment A[1], attached hereto or as such form may be modified from time to time. The parties may by mutual written agreement modify, alter, or amend the SOW.

Additional Projects or services may be issued by CUSTOMER pursuant to new or additional SOWs, and upon acceptance by CONSULTANT shall be governed by this Agreement and incorporated in and made a part of this Agreement.

CONSULTANT shall undertake and accomplish the project with standards and expectations acceptable to CUSTOMER as identified in the SOW. In carrying out the Project, CONSULTANT shall maintain liaison with such CUSTOMER partner or manager as CUSTOMER may designate.

Independent Contractor Status

CONSULTANT shall be an independent contractor and CONSULTANT acknowledges, and confirms to CUSTOMER its status as that of an independent contractor. Nothing herein shall be deemed or construed to create a joint venture, partnership, agency, or employee / employer relationship between the two

---

[1] Attachment A, the Statement of Work, is not illustrated in this model contract. For information see page 24.

employer relationship between the two parties for any purpose, including but not limited to taxes or employee benefits. CONSULTANT shall be solely responsible for payment of any and all taxes and for its own insurance coverage.

Power to Act on Behalf of CUSTOMER

CONSULTANT shall not have any right, power, or authority to create any obligation, express or implied, or make representation on behalf of CUSTOMER except as CONSULTANT may be expressly authorized from time to time by CUSTOMER and then only to the extent of such authorization.

Fees

Professional fees for services will be billed based on the actual hours worked plus actual incurred out-of-pocket expenses. Estimated professional fees for this project are specified in the attached Statement of Work (SOW). CUSTOMER and CONSULTANT will mutually agree on workdays. CONSULTANT shall not be entitled to any other compensation for this Project.

CONSULTANT will submit invoices at least monthly. CUSTOMER shall pay invoices within thirty (30) days of receipt.

Expenses

CUSTOMER shall reimburse CONSULTANT for out-of-pocket expenses, which will be billed at actual amounts incurred in connection with CONSULTANT's project, such as travel, lodging, communications, project supplies and aids. CUSTOMER shall pay invoices within thirty (30) days of receipt.

Choosing and Using a Consultant

CONSULTANT shall maintain records relating to CONSULTANT's Project and to expenses incurred in connection therewith and shall provide CUSTOMER access to such records upon request during normal business hours.

CONSULTANT's Covenants

CONSULTANT covenants to CUSTOMER as follows:

A. CONSULTANT will comply at all times with all applicable laws and regulations of any jurisdiction in which CONSULTANT acts;

B. CONSULTANT will comply with all applicable CUSTOMER policies and standards and will carry out the Project in a manner consistent with the ethical and professional standards of CUSTOMER;

C. CONSULTANT will comply with all security provisions in effect from time to time at CUSTOMER premises;

D. CONSULTANT shall not use CUSTOMER's name in any promotional materials or other communications with third parties without CUSTOMER's prior written consent;

E. CONSULTANT is legally authorized to engage in business in the United States and will provide CUSTOMER satisfactory evidence of such authority upon request;

Choosing and Using a Consultant

F. If the CUSTOMER requires, CONSULTANT will complete periodic formal project status reports.

Ownership

Ownership rights to work product created by CONSULTANT hereunder and conferred upon CUSTOMER by the terms of this Agreement, including the Statement of Work incorporated herein, shall become the property of CUSTOMER[2].

Confidentiality

During the course of carrying out the Project, CONSULTANT may have access to information that (i) relates to CUSTOMER's past, present, or future re-search, development, or business activities and to pro-prietary products, materials, services, or technical knowledge, and (ii) is regarded as confidential by CUSTOMER ("Confidential Information"). In connec-tion therewith, the following subsections shall apply:

---

[2] Some consultants may object to giving the cus-tomer ownership of everything created during a project. There is some justice to their objections since the provision effectively prevents them from embedding proprietary work that they already own in the work performed under the agreement. Fur-ther it should be recognized that consultants are constantly interested in leveraging work done for one client to better serve the next one. If the con-sultant objects, you might consider modifying the language to limit it to only those items that you consider proprietary to your business.

39

Choosing and Using a Consultant

A. The Confidential Information may be used by CONSULTANT only to assist CONSULTANT in connection with the Project;

B. CONSULTANT will protect the confidentiality of the Confidential Information in the same manner that CONSULTANT protects his own confidential information of like kind. Access to the Confidential Information shall be restricted to CONSULTANT and CUSTOMER's personnel and CONSULTANT shall not disclose Confidential Information to any third party;

C. Unless otherwise expressly authorized in writing by CUSTOMER, all Confidential Information made available to CONSULTANT, including copies thereof, shall be returned to CUSTOMER upon the first to occur of (i) termination of this Agreement or (ii) request by CUSTOMER; and

D. Nothing in this Agreement shall prohibit or limit CONSULTANT's use of information (including, but not limited to ideas, concepts, know-how, techniques, and methodology) (i) previously known to him, (ii) independently developed by him, (iii) acquired by him from a third party which is not, to CONSULTANT's knowledge, under an obligation to CUSTOMER not to disclose such information, or (iv) which is or becomes publicly available through no breach by CONSULTANT of this Agreement.

Choosing and Using a Consultant

Indemnification

CONSULTANT shall indemnify and hold CUSTOMER, its partners, employees, and agents, harmless from and against any claims, demands, loss, damage, or expense (i) related to bodily injury or death of any person or damage to property resulting from the negligent or willful acts or omissions of CONSULTANT, (ii) resulting from any claim that CONSULTANT is not an independent contractor, except where claim is the result of negligence by CUSTOMER, (iii) incurred by CUSTOMER based on any claim that any deliverable or other materials delivered under this Agreement or use thereof by CUSTOMER infringes any copyright, trade secret, or other proprietary right of any third party, or (iv) resulting from a breach by CONSULTANT of the covenants listed above.

Limitation of Liability

Neither party shall be liable to the other party for any indirect, incidental, special, or consequential damages (including, without limitation, any damages arising from loss of use or lost business, revenue, profits, data, or goodwill) arising in connection with this Agreement, whether in an action in contract, tort, strict liability, or negligence, even if advised of the possibility of such damages. IN ALL EVENTS, CONSULTANT'S LIABILITY UNDER THIS AGREEMENT SHALL BE LIMITED TO THE AMOUNT PAID BY CUSTOMER TO CONSULTANT.

The provisions of this Section shall survive the termination or cancellation of this Agreement.

Choosing and Using a Consultant

Term

This agreement shall be effective as of the date hereof and shall continue for so long as CONSULTANT is performing services for CUSTOMER, unless the scope of the agreement is extended pursuant to express written agreement of the parties.

Termination

CUSTOMER or CONSULTANT may terminate this Agreement with or without cause at any time by delivering written notice of termination to the other party at the address given above.

In the event this agreement is terminated, CONSULTANT shall be entitled to payment of all fees and reimbursement of expenses incurred prior to the effective date of such termination.

Upon termination of this agreement for any reason, CONSULTANT will cease all activity for CUSTOMER and shall promptly provide to CUSTOMER, without cost to CUSTOMER, all work product and files developed by CONSULTANT under this Agreement and all materials provided to CONSULTANT by CUSTOMER in connection with this Agreement.

Successors and Assigns

This agreement shall be binding upon, and inure to the benefit of the parties hereto and their respective successors, permitted assigns and legal representatives, including without limitation a purchaser of a majority of all or substantially all of the assets of either party. Nothing in this agreement is intended to confer any rights or remedies on any person or entity that is not a party to this agreement. Neither this agreement nor any right or obligation hereunder may be assigned, transferred, or delegated, voluntarily or by operation of law, by either party hereto without the prior written consent of the other party hereto; provided that no such consent shall be necessary for such an assignment, transfer or delegation by either party to an affiliate or successor by way of merger, consolidation, or sale of all or substantially all of such party's outstanding voting securities or assets.

Governing Law

This Agreement shall be governed by and construed in accordance with the laws of the State of _____, without giving effect to the principles of conflicts of laws thereof. The parties agree that in the event a dispute arises between them and cannot be resolved between the two parties themselves that their exclusive remedy shall be to submit the dispute to the American Arbitration Association, for binding arbitration before a single arbitrator. The parties shall share equally in the expenses of the arbitration but shall bear their own attorney fees and costs.

Complete Agreement

This Agreement sets forth the entire understanding and agreement of the parties as to the provision of consulting services by CONSULTANT to CUSTOMER. It may not be changed orally but only in writing signed by both parties.

Document Expiration

This proposed Agreement expires in _____ business days from the date of record, noted below in the Acceptance. CONSULTANT must receive signed acceptance

Choosing and Using a Consultant

on or before the expiration date, or the proposed agreement becomes void.

IN WITNESS WHEREOF, the parties have duly exe-
cuted this Agreement as of the day and year first above
written.

Agreed to and accepted by

	Consultant	Customer
Signature	_____	_____
Printed Name		
Date	_____	_____
Date of record	_____	

www.ingramcontent.com/pod-product-compliance
Lightning Source LLC
Chambersburg PA
CBHW030011190526
45157CB00015B/2306